Tapping into Your Superpower

Table of Contents

Preface

All Christians have a superpower, but many have not yet tapped into it.

Many superheroes require a place or point of contact to unleash their power. The Power Rangers say: "It's morphing time! Activate Beast Powers!" Diana Prince does a pirouette and transforms into Wonder Woman; Clark Kent uses a telephone booth to turn into Superman; Peter Parker, having been bitten by a radioactive spider, gains super abilities and becomes Spider-Man.

For the post-quarantine Christian, prayer is our superpower.

Prayer is our superpower. Furthermore, there is superpower inside every Christian that requires activation through prayer. Thus, prayer operates on two levels: it is both a manifestation of our superpower and further lends itself to releasing other Holy Spirit powers in us.

Prayer is our superpower because when we pray, we pray to a sovereign God who can do supernatural exploits for our supreme good. In essence, our prayers request God to activate His power on our behalf. Then, it functions to allow God to stir us to do great exploits for the empowerment of others and for the good of our communities.

The busyness of life often inhibits our ability to activate and unleash our superpower. The ebb and flow of daily experiences can distance us from God. Prayer is not passive discourse but powerful petition to a merciful God who can change the situation and change us. Prayer, rather, mobilizes us for mission.

Prayer was a superpower that mobilized the Civil Rights Movement. Some of the most powerful images from the movement show Dr. King and protestors kneeling in prayer before rallies and sit-ins. Although demonstrators were greeted with violence, prayer kept their hearts turned to God so that persistent, peaceful protests against racial injustice moved a nation to repent and enact just laws.

Furthermore, prayer is a counter narrative, which deconstructs and delegitimizes narratives that oppress, marginalize, dehumanize, detract, and distract from Kingdom impetus. Prayer is not a last resort nor a cop-out nor a weakness. Prayer is really one of the most powerful spiritual weapons we possess as Christians because prayer, motivated by the Holy-Spirit, really invites God into our lives and contexts. Through prayer, we invite God to change mindsets that are more politically oriented rather than biblically oriented; through prayer, we invite God into spaces that are still dark and require light; through prayer, we invite God to bring flavor to the blandness of our communal discourses and behavior, especially when they are not in tandem with Kingdom agenda.

Finally, prayer is such a powerful way to participate in making the world a better place. Our hope is that this devotional will inspire you, help you to recognize and respond to your superpower ability, and tap into it habitually to fully unleash it so that the Kingdom of God may fully come in your life, family, and contexts.

Superpowers activate!

- Joanne J. Noel

A Life Seasoned with Grace

"Prayer is the believer's privilege."

Grace matters to God. That is why there is an abundance of grace available to cover the vilest of transgressions. Like praying is our superpower because we have this divine, unconditional access to the presence of God who hears our prayers and will answer according to His will, so Grace is one of God's superpowers. John 3:16 is the perfect illustration of grace in action: "For God so loved the world that he gave his only begotten son that whoever believes in him would not perish but have everlasting life." The text effervesces with God's grace. The effect of God's giving of His son sacrificially, once and for all, for the sin of all humanity was rooted in His love for us. We did not deserve such a magnanimous display of affection, but such a display is a testament to the favor that God bestows on His beloved.

A Prayer for Preaching of the Gospel

Holy Father, position humanity to be eternally blessed. Cause, O God, revival to take place in the land through the preaching and hearing of the Gospel of Jesus Christ. May the young and old, rich and poor, people from various political parties and from all ethnic groups, tongues, creeds and nationalities hear and heed Your message of salvation. And in hearing produce in us a spirit of repentance and confession. May we turn away from sin and embrace the Savior. Amen.

A Prayer for Salvation

Father, like the gushing forth of water from a waterfall, I pray for salvation to flow all over the world. Amen.

A Prayer for Deliverance

Dear Father, may your people be delivered. Correct any disorder in our lives, bodies, businesses, places of employment, ministries, and relationships. Heal the sick. Bring peace to the distressed. Comfort the broken-hearted. Strengthen the weary. Lift up the fallen. In Jesus' name, Amen.

<u>A Prayer for the Indwelling of the Holy Spirit</u>

Loving Father, our lives are in Your hands. Stretch out in us, Holy Spirit. Bless us with the fruit of the Spirit. Bless us with the gifts of the Spirit. Position us for and in purpose. May Your power and presence go before us. May Your grace overflow in us. Use us for Your honor and glory. Your kingdom come on earth. Your will be done in our life. In Jesus' name, Amen.

Tapping into My Superpower

MY PRAYER PETITION

_____

_____

_____

_____

_____

_____

The Matters of the Kingdom

"Prayer warriors are essential workers."

An X-factor is defined as a variable in a given situation that could have the most significant impact on the outcome. The X-factor for believers is the "God-factor": our trust in God who is at work in our lives. When we allow God to direct our paths, our perspectives change, and the outcome changes to optimally benefit us. Romans 8:28 says, "And we know that in all things God works for the good of those who love him, who have been called according to his purpose." On the path of life, sometimes, we don't need God to tell us all the details. Sometimes, all we need to do is trust God in the move. We don't always need to understand but obey. Leave room for the mystery of God and the strengthening of your faith. Trust implies confidence, and confidence implies a healthy relationship.

We don't have a relationship with people we don't trust. Trust is the cornerstone of a healthy relationship. Some have referred to it as the glue of a relationship, without which relationships don't last. For the post quarantine Christian, it's a no-brainer to put trust in the Omniscient Creator of the universe who knows the future. Nothing can take God by surprise, so for the church, the X-factor is trust. Trust undergirds the superpower of prayer.

A Prayer for Trust

Holy Spirit, fill our hearts with light and love. Align our wills with Yours. Teach us to trust in You with all our hearts. Direct us with Your divine compass. Amen.

A Prayer for the Indwelling of the Holy Spirit

Stretch out in us, Holy Spirit. Let us decrease and Your power and presence increase in us. Stir up Your gifts in us. Inundate us with the fruits of the Spirit. Use us for Your honor and glory. Make us instruments of Your peace. Where there is hatred, let us show love. Amen.

A Prayer to Do Kingdom Work

You are the all-knowing and merciful One. You are the hope for nations, the wellspring of life. We are no longer our own, but Yours. We have been bought with a price, purchased by the precious blood of Jesus Christ. For You have loved us with an everlasting love, and with loving kindness, You have called us unto Yourself. Forgive us of our sins, shortcomings, failures, inconsistencies, and proclivities. Fill us with Your Holy Spirit. Use us for Your honor and glory. Put us to work as You wish. Put us in the places you desire, for the work of your kingdom. Amen.

A Prayer to be Conformed into the Image of Jesus

Keep our mind on You. Help us to see as You see, to be concerned with the things that concern You, O holy Father. Draw us closer to You. Let us know You and the fellowship of Your sufferings. Deliver us from evil thoughts and vain imaginations. Conform us into the image of Your son, Jesus. Transform us by the renewing of our minds.

For Christian Workers

The harvest is plentiful, but the laborers are few. Send laborers to Your work. Strengthen the few who are weary. For persecuted Christians to find joy and deliverance amid suffering, we pray.

A Prayer for Boldness

May Christians everywhere know Your peace, Your joy, and Your love and unity, for Christians to love one another. We pray for churches everywhere to be about our Father's business. Give us boldness to tell people that Jesus is Savior, we pray. Give us courage to share the Gospel, we pray. Amen.

A Prayer for Unity

God, the church is Your business. Deliver us from the spirit of offense. Help us to be quick to forgive. Deliver us from schisms, pride, and cantankerousness. May we always strive for unity that helps us stay focused on Your work, for Your glory. Amen.

A Prayer for an Attitude of Forgiveness

Father, change our attitudes so that we can forgive easily those who have offended us. Help us to release them so that we may have the kind of peace that allows us to go on with life. Give us the strength to be committed to the process of change. Amen.

A Prayer for Deliverance

Father, deliver us from a haughty spirit. Holy Spirit convict us when we are the ones who have caused contention. Teach us how to say, "I am sorry," when we have wronged someone. Amen.

A Prayer for Liberation

Healing God, deliver us from the pain and anger that we have experienced because of hurts, abuses, and betrayals. Deliver us from replaying those events in our minds. Deliver us from the turmoil and the tyranny of the trauma. Help us to let go of resentment and thoughts of revenge. We pray for cleansing and healing, in Jesus' name.

A Prayer of Releasing

Merciful God, we release those who have wronged us. And we pray that those whom we have wronged, willfully or unintentionally, release us from their minds and hearts. Amen.

A Prayer for Resources

Blessed Father, who owns the cattle on a thousand hills, the earth is Yours and its fullness. Please bless us with the provisions we need to do ministry effectively. Amen.

A Prayer for Revival

Bring revival in our villages. Bring revival in our cities. Bring revival in our states. Bring revival in our nations. Let there be a bold preaching and teaching of Your Word. Let Your Holy Spirit descend on us like tongues of flaming fire. Amen.

A Prayer for the Coming of God's Kingdom

Let Your kingdom come on earth, in our lives, in the lives of our families, our churches, our communities, and our countries. Loving and forgiving God, You are our Father, and we belong to You. We love You. As we joyfully await the coming of our Lord and Savior, Jesus the Christ, we ask that You lead, guide, direct, protect and govern us. As we await the return of Jesus, strengthen us to be better disciples. For Yours, O Holy Father, is the kingdom, the power and the glory. In Jesus' name, we pray. Amen.

Tapping into My Superpower

MY PRAYER PETITION

_____

_____

_____

_____

_____

_____

_____

_____

_____

_____

_____

_____

A Way with Words

"The posture of prayer is a winning posture."

Putting a smiley face next to harsh words doesn't make them less vitriolic, just like putting sugar in poison wouldn't make death sweeter. James 3:6 points to the arbitrary and ungodly ways in which we speak that weaken our testimony. He notes:

The tongue also is a fire, a world of evil among the parts of the body. It corrupts the whole person, sets the whole course of his life on fire, and is itself set on fire by hell. All kinds of animals, birds, reptiles, and creatures of the sea are being tamed and have been tamed by man, but no man can tame the tongue. It is a restless evil, full of deadly poison. With the tongue we praise our Lord and Father, and with it we curse men, who have been made in God's likeness. Out of the same mouth come praise and cursing. My brothers, this should not be.

Some of us have a way with using words. Our words can be thoughtless, insensitive, and unkind. Of course, there are contexts in which stern words are required, but contrary to what Shakespeare said, we don't always have to "be cruel to be kind." One way to combat this behavior is to recognize our triggers (those situations that would cause us to speak in ugly ways) and learn to control ourselves in such situations. That is, we should always think before we speak; walk away from the person or situation; don't send the e-mail responding to a negative situation on the same day; say a quick prayer. And even when the situation requires us to respond immediately, use our self-edit and delete buttons. Words are powerful, and we ought to use this power wisely in positive life-giving ways.

A Prayer for Wisdom with Words

Holy Spirit, I pray for wisdom in my word choices. I pray the words of Isaiah 50:4, "The Lord GOD hath given me the tongue of the learned, that I should know how to speak a word in season to him/her that is weary." Give us wisdom to know not only what the right thing to say is, but also the right time

*on when to say it so that it can bless people
and make a difference. Amen.*

A Prayer for Self- Control

*Father, I realize that it is out of the heart
that the mouth speaks. Purify me from the
inside out. May Your Holy Spirit refine me.
Inundate me with the fruit of the Spirit; bless
me with self-control. Make and mold me into
the image of my Savior, Jesus. Amen.*

A Prayer for Purification

*Lord, purify my tongue. Put a gate around
the door of my mouth. Let words that bless
come forth. Let words that heal prevail.
Amen.*

A Prayer for Reversal

*Holy Spirit, I pray for forgiveness for the
terrible things I have said to others. Please
reverse all the problems I have caused with
my mouth. Even now sanctify my tongue and
use me to speak words of life. Amen.*

<u>A Prayer to Speak</u>

Lord, help me to use my tongue to speak empowerment to my students; to speak life, health, and wealth to my congregation; to speak respectfully and kindly to my neighbors. Help me always to speak the truth in love and to never be afraid to speak truth in power. Amen.

Tapping into My Superpower

MY PRAYER PETITION

_____

_____

_____

_____

_____

_____

_____

The Value of Godly Women

"Prayer takes us through the portal of everyday worries into the majestic presence of the Mighty."

A critical examination of the experiences of some women has led me to conclude that one's value does not decrease based on someone's inability to see one's worth. The immediate value of some sisters has been obscured by principalities and powers that relegated them to the margins, rendered them invisible, silenced their voices, and refused them a seat at the table. Yet, the reason we know their value is that they refused to embrace the devaluing by these principalities and powers. Their spirits refused to be trampled and rose to majestic heights of splendor. Women like Jarena Lee, Elizabeth Cady Stanton, Esther, Bernadette Glover, Deborah, Mary of Magdalene, Mary the mother of Jesus, Cicely Tyson, Fannie Lou Hamer, Oprah Winfrey, my mother, and some of my women colleagues/academicians and sister clergywomen, whether in the spotlight or obscure, have demonstrated the tenacity of the spider. Despite challenges and setbacks encountered in academia, the church, and the marketplace, they have demonstrated resilience.

A Prayer for Women in Leadership

Strengthen women leaders everywhere. May they not be discouraged and turn back but keep pressing forward. Provide the physical, psychological, and spiritual stamina they need. Provide the resources they need. Give them insight and strategies. Bless them with the ability to plan, implement, and execute. Put the right teams around them. Give them discernment so that they know when to pursue, take risks, or stand still. May they lead according to the direction of the Holy Spirit. Amen.

A Prayer for Businesswomen

God, I pray for businesswomen everywhere, that You will strengthen their resolves. I pray that You will bless them with creative and innovative ideas. Cause them to prosper and take their businesses to the next level. Help them to attract the right employees. May employees provide a fair day's work for a fair day's pay. May employees not be abused, mistreated, and disadvantaged but treated with an ethic of care. May the right environment be created so that employees will feel valued. Amen.

A Prayer for Women in Academia

God, thank You for bringing us through and bringing us over. We pray for perseverance to get our various degrees, strength to overcome the obstacles, opportunities to teach, present, and empower, creativity to write and favor to publish. Deliver us from unhealthy competitiveness. Deliver us from unholy expectations. Keep us from sabotages and the tricks and schemes of the devil. Keep us from workplace bullying, racism, and sexism. Help us to partner with You to grow in grace. Help us to give our fullest and highest to You. Amen.

A Prayer for Women Called to Ministry

Holy Father, You are able. Thank You for calling us to Your service. And now, we call upon the God who is able:

- *Able to do exceedingly abundantly above all we ask or think.*
- *Able to deliver us, keep us, comfort us, correct us.*
- *Able to protect us, provide for us, open doors for us.*
- *Able to remove obstacles from our paths.*
- *Able to right wrongs.*
- *Able to shatter glass ceilings.*
- *Able to give us favor.*

We thank You, in Jesus' name.

A Prayer for Women Training for Ministry

Dear Father, please provide us with the resources we need to do ministry effectively. Send us to the right schools. Give us access to good theological and ministry programs. Place us in environments of grace where we will grow. Bless us with good, godly instructors. Amen.

A Prayer for a Servant's Heart for Women in Ministry

Holy God, we pray for the right ministry attitude. We desire a spirit of humility. Remind us that those who want to lead are called to be servants. Imbue us with a servant's heart. Amen.

A Prayer for the Fruits of the Spirit for Women in Ministry

Father, fill us with the fruits of the Spirit: joy, love, peace, long-suffering, faithfulness, gentleness, meekness, self-restraint, and long-suffering. Amen.

A Prayer for Continued Growth for Women in Ministry

Loving Father, may we gain knowledge and wisdom from the books we read and may what we learn empower us to serve effectively. Gracious God, may we sit at the feet of good mentors and learn and grow in grace. Bless us with good mentors. Amen.

A Prayer for Healthy Marriages and Peaceful Homes for Women in Ministry

Father, remember our spouses. Thank You for the covenant of marriage, for the strong men You have placed in our lives to journey with us. Thank You for the high priests of our homes. May we always treat them with dignity, respect, and love. May whatever difficulties we may have in the home never be inappropriately used in sermons. Help us to seek marital counseling when necessary. Help us to be quick to forgive any offense. Heal any breaches in our homes and in our marriages. Anoint our laps for our husbands' heads. Watch over our spouses and keep them from harm and danger. God, sanctify our mouths so that words which instruct, edify, correct, encourage, and inspire may come forth.

A Prayer for Strength for Women in Ministry

Father, help us so that we never become stumbling blocks to someone's faith walk. Teach us to pray as You taught Your disciples. Give us strength to face every struggle that comes our way. Help us to be overcomers. Amen.

A Prayer for First Ladies in the Church

Loving Father, as You have called the spouses of these women, so have You called these women with a holy calling. Anoint their hands to bring comfort to their spouses. Anoint their lips to speak truth and love and kindness. May their laps be consecrated to shelter the heads of their spouses. Keep them from the whiplash of gossip and character assassination. May they never cause division and contention in the church. May they never join with others to malign their spouses. May they treat their spouses with integrity, kindness, and respect. May their spouses treat them with integrity, kindness, and respect. May they treat all members with dignity and respect. May they always provide healthy leadership.

Put a hedge of protection around them. May they be good mothers to their children. May they be praying women. May they be brave women. May they be Holy-Spirit filled women. May they grow in grace. Keep a watchful eye over them and, in Your kind care, keep them from all harm, dangers, and accidents. In Jesus' name. Amen.

Tapping into My Superpower

MY PRAYER PETITION

_____

_____

_____

_____

_____

_____

_____

_____

Families Matter to God

"The best prayer is Thy will be done."

God loves kin. Family is God's design.
God saved Lot not because he was a
righteous man (we know he was not) but
because, as recorded in Genesis 19:29, God
remembered the intercessory prayer of
Abraham and saved Lot and his family. Lot
was Abraham's nephew. You see, God was
so angry with the wicked people of Sodom
and Gomorrah that He was going to destroy
them all. Abraham understood that God was
justified but sought to appeal to God's
mercy first by drawing a circle of about fifty
people around Lot, and then forty-five,
forty, thirty—the circle getting tighter
because there were no righteous people.

It can be a lonely walk through life if you
are the first, and seemingly the only one,
saved in your immediate and extended
family. Your all-consuming desire is to see
your loved ones experience the joy and
freedom of salvation and to have their
names written in that Book of Life and

counted as righteous. Beloved, stay consistent in your witness, bold in your testimony, loving in your approach, and fervent in your prayers. In fact, tap deeply into the superpower of prayers. God loves kin, and He will hear your prayers.

A Prayer for Sons, Daughters, Nieces/Nephews, and Grandchildren

God of salvation, as You heard the prayer of Abraham and saved Lot, hear our prayers for our kin and save them, too. Free them from the lust of the flesh, the lust of the eyes, and the pride of life. We pray for (name them here) that they may experience the joy of knowing You and the victory of trusting in You. In the name of Jesus, Amen.

A Prayer for Healing

Healing God, please deliver my child from the ravages of this disease. May every tissue, ligament, organ, cell, and vessel in my child's body line up with the Word of God. By Your stripes, he/she is healed. Amen.

A Prayer for Deliverance from Addiction

Merciful Lord, deliver my daughter/son/ nephew/niece from every form of addiction that seduces him/her and spiritually and mentally impoverishes him/her. May he/she lead a whole, healthy, and God-glorifying life. Amen.

A Prayer against Temptation

Holy Father, it seems everywhere we look these days, there is the lust of the flesh, the lust of the eyes, and the pride of life. Deliver my children from temptation and teach them to hide Your Word in their hearts so that they do not sin against you. Lead them in paths of truth. Amen.

A Prayer for Wisdom to Live Right

Loving Savior, please grant my children wisdom to make healthy and good life choices and decisions. Deliver them from the negative consequences of ungodly choices. Have mercy on them. Amen.

A Prayer for Good Jobs and Careers

Father, please bless my children with the right jobs and the right careers. Grant them favor. Amen.

A Thank You Prayer

Lord, thank You for the blessings of peace, joy, love, favor, and prosperity over my family. You have been good to us and for that we sing Your praises. Amen

Tapping into My Superpower

MY PRAYER PETITION

_____

_____

_____

_____

_____

_____

_____

Let Children Come to God

"Prayer is not magic. It's 'mighty through God for the uprooting and pulling down of strongholds.'"

The calling of the prophet Samuel brings us face-to-face with an aging father, the priest Eli, whose sons had somehow lost their way. Because of his wayward children, Eli does not stand out as a good father. It is not known what possessed the mother of Samuel to entrust her precious little boy to this man who had seemingly failed to raise his own children to know, love, and serve the God that he had served all his life. And yet, even in the twilight of his life, it seems Eli knew enough to recognize the calling of God—so much so that he was able to coach the lad Samuel through his own calling. Perhaps Samuel was not only an answer to Hannah's prayer but also a reminder to Eli that God's mercy endures. The Psalmist declares in Psalm 103:17, "… but the mercy of the Lord is from everlasting to everlasting upon them that fear Him and His righteousness to his children's children."

A Prayer for Strength to Raise Godly Children

Holy Father, Your Word says that we should "train up children in the way they should go, and when they are old, they will not depart from it." Would You now please give me the strength I need to raise my children in faith? Help me to raise them to value godliness, to be good neighbors, to love God, to love people, to serve with integrity, to be healthy citizens, and to pursue godly justice. In Jesus' name, I pray. Amen.

A Prayer for Children in Cults

Dear God, my weapons are not carnal but mighty through You. I, therefore, cast down every imagination and false teaching, every thought and idea that has obscured Your truth and the knowledge of YOU. We pray that the hearts and minds of our children are now free to know Christ and Him crucified. Amen.

A Prayer for Children Who Have Left the Church

Father, in Your presence there is fullness of joy, and at Your right hand there are pleasures forevermore. Cause our children to remember and yearn for the joy, the peace, the hope of being found in the Body of Christ. In His Name we pray, Amen.

A Prayer for Children the Church has Ostracized

Dear God, sometimes the Church confuses holiness with condemnation. Forgive us for forgetting that we are all sinners saved by grace and for casting stones at those we should be lovingly showing the way to mercy. Pour salve on those we have wounded and bring them back home to You. Amen.

A Prayer for the Children of Pastors

The enemy knows when he captures the hearts of the children of Your servants that he distracts Your servants from Your work. I pray for the children of Your servants. As they are busy doing Your business, shield, defend, and save their children so that Your servants will not be ashamed nor the enemy triumph over them. Amen.

A Thank You Prayer

Loving Father, help us to never lose sight of the truth that children are a gift from You; procreation and parenting are an undeserved glimpse into Your original plan in Eden. Thank You for the opportunity to cast our hopes into the future through our children. Amen.

Tapping into My Superpower
MY PRAYER PETITION

_____

_____

_____

_____

_____

_____

_____

_____

_____

_____

_____

_____

_____

Even the Best Dads have Prodigal Sons

"Prayer softens a wayward heart and reins in a wayward mind."

True to the scriptures, "the father of a righteous child has great joy; a man who fathers a wise son rejoices in him" (Prov. 23:24). The opposite is also true. Far from the usual "You are the best Dad" cards, this year I gave my husband a scripture card. In the last couple of years, I have witnessed my husband hurt and worry about our son's wasted opportunities. As long as there is time to turn around (the prodigal son in the Bible did turn around), we have got to believe that our son will "come to his senses" because surely God is well able to turn the hearts of the fathers to their children and the hearts of the children to their fathers (Mal. 4:6). Our task is to wait with open arms. Over and over, God has done it for us. May we never lose sight of the God of many chances.

A Prayer for Wayward Children

Abba—Daddy—You whose idea it is to be a parent, I take hold of Your promise and hold tightly to Your everlasting mercy. Forgive the times when I, like Eli, may not have been that exemplary parent. In Your mercy and righteousness, I commit my children back to You. Set the hounds of Heaven upon them to chase them back to me and most importantly back to You and to the way of salvation. In the name of Your precious Son, I pray, Amen.

A Prayer for Patience and Grace for Our Children

Father of many prodigals, God of many chances, Your example is to never give up. You keep on loving us even when we disappoint You. Help us to be joyful in hope, patient in affliction, and faithful in prayer for our sons/daughters. In your Son's Name, Amen

A Prayer for Forgiveness

Father, forgive me for the times I may have acted in ways or said words to provoke (embitter) my children to anger and caused them discouragement. Grant me the courage and humility to ask for their forgiveness and give them the grace to forgive me. Reconcile their hearts to mine and mine to theirs. For your sake, Amen.

A Prayer for Disappointed Children

Healer of broken hearts, sometimes the source of disappointment is the mother or father who did not know or did not try to parent as they should have. For the children who have been bewildered, wounded, and perhaps callously neglected, abandoned, or even abused—we pray for the Balm of Gilead, the only One who can cut through the scars and heal the wounded heart. Bring these children back to You. Amen.

A Thank You Prayer

Abba, Thank You for the honor of being called "Daddy" and for the love, honor, and obedience of my children. I am grateful for the godly generation coming after me. I know, it is only by Your grace that that is so. Help me never to take it for granted. Amen

Tapping into My Superpower

MY PRAYER PETITION

_____

_____

_____

_____

_____

_____

_____

_____

Unequally Yoked?

**"Even a whispered prayer is strong
enough to break the toughest chain."**

The Apostle Paul commands the Church
at Corinth: *Do not be yoked together with
unbelievers. For what do righteousness and
wickedness have in common? Or what
fellowship can light have with darkness?* (2
Cor. 6:14). Single Christians cannot tell you
how many times Youth and Senior Pastors
repeat this admonition for fear that these
young, marriageable men and women might
slip up and fall in love with a 'non-believer.'
The fear is not without merit.

Yet, tucked away among the God's
Prophets is one Hosea, who was
commanded to do the exact opposite. As an
illustration for the harlotry of the people of
God, God tells Hosea to marry a harlot, a
promiscuous woman—a bad girl. It is easy
to read portions of the book of Hosea and
say, "How could God do such a thing to His
faithful servant?" However, the rest of
Hosea is about God falling in love again and

not only restoring but also redeeming His people back to Himself. The 'not my people' becomes 'my people,' the 'not my wife/husband' becomes 'my husband/wife,' the 'children of harlotry' become 'sons/daughters of the Living God.' The lesson to Israel/Judah and Hosea is that mercy is a prerequisite to reconciliation.

A Prayer for a Spouse's Salvation

Great Savior, Your Word invites me to believe in the Lord Jesus and I will be saved—me and my entire household. I am believing You for the salvation of my husband/wife (insert name here). I long for the day he/she and I will, together, look joyfully to the glorious day of Your second coming. Amen.

A Prayer to Separate our Children from Evil Company

Almighty God, a good child can turn bad by choosing bad friends. By Your Holy Spirit, help us to influence the friends our children pick, and as they grow, help them to see into the character of those around them so that they may make wise and godly choices in the company they keep.

A Prayer for Godly Life Partners

Lord, please bless my sons and daughters with godly spouses. May their choices of life partners be pleasing in Your eyes. And, likewise, prepare my sons and daughters to be the godly spouses other godly men and women will be attracted to. In the precious name of Jesus, Amen

A Thank You Prayer

Loving God, thank You for reconciling us to Yourself through Your son Jesus Christ, and us to one another by Your grace and power. Amen.

Tapping into My Superpower

MY PRAYER PETITION

_____

_____

_____

_____

_____

_____

_____

_____

_____

_____

_____

_____

A Kinsman Redeemer

"Prayer is water for the thirsty and bread for the hungry, and so, we pray because there is never a famine of the mercies of God."

Joseph was scandalized by Mary's out-of-wedlock pregnancy. Nevertheless, because he had no interest in shaming Mary, the Bible records him as a righteous man. We are allowed a window into Mary's story right from the angel's visitation, so we are fine with the blessed and holy event. In most circumstances, regardless of how it happened, an out-of-wedlock pregnancy, for most Christian families, throws the hopes and dreams of the family into disarray. The family experiences something akin to grief. Somewhere between shock and acceptance, there is also shame and embarrassment. *What will people say?* Righteous one, God has His eye on your seed. If His plan includes marriage, in His time, He will send a Boaz or a Joseph, a righteous man to walk this journey with your daughter, or a godly woman to walk with your son. Indeed, God Himself has already paid the price by sending His own child to die for ours. The price is already paid. He is our Go'el—our Kinsman Redeemer. Keep your eyes on God and keep loving your child.

A Prayer for God to Redeem Order

God of time, season, and order, only You can reorder that which has fallen out of sequence. Only You can redeem us from our sense of disappointment and shame. Help us to keep our eyes on the miracle of conception and birth—the miracle of new life. Thank You for the gift of grandchildren and the knowledge that their time of arrival is in Your hands. If You will, when You will, we know You will send a kinsman redeemer as You did for Ruth and Mary. Amen.

A Prayer of Reconciliation in Families

The timing of the arrival of our grandchildren may not have been expected or planned but help us to set aside our plans and expectations to embrace life and the privilege of seeing our children's children.

Help us to be an influence of righteousness for this next generation. Amen.

A Prayer for our Children to Find the Right Spouses

Father, we ask for righteous, loving, and kind spouses for our sons/daughters. Someone who will love our son/daughter without reservation; one who will adopt and raise our grandchildren lovingly as his/her own, and one who will intercede for the family and seek to walk in Your will. Amen.

A Prayer of Adoption for Children Needing a Forever Home

Father, our hearts bleed for the many children in unloving foster homes, cruel orphanages, mean and cold streets, and teen homeless shelters. Grant every child that longs for a loving forever family, a forever family. Amen.

Tapping into My Superpower

MY PRAYER PETITION

_____

_____

_____

_____

_____

_____

_____

_____

_____

_____

_____

_____

_____

God's Loving Kindness

"Praying preserves the faithful."

God hates divorce…Period. At least, that is what it says in Malachi 2:16, *"For the LORD God of Israel says That He hates divorce, for it covers one's garment with violence. Therefore, take heed to your spirit that you do not deal treacherously."* This statement falls like a ton of bricks over the heads of Christians who find themselves in circumstances of divorce. And yet…no one in their right mind, not even God, allows for people to stay in circumstances of emotional and physical abuse, neglect, or abandonment. The Bible gives an out (Ex. 21:10-11; I Tim 5:8). Hosea found it necessary to "put away" Gomer until commanded to redeem her to himself again. Divorced families are still families. Hosea and Gomer and their children were a family. The God who hates divorce would prefer reconciliation—provided there is true remorse. In the absence of that and an assurance of safety and providence, He would rather have safety. Trust that He is well able to meet all material, emotional, and spiritual needs.

A Prayer for Redemption

El Kanna, though You are a jealous God, You are also Elohim Chesdi/Cheseddi. Your loving kindness is better than life itself. It redeems, mends, and restores that which is broken. Keep us always close to Your heart. Amen.

A Prayer for Healing from a Broken Heart

Redeemer of Judah and Israel, because You show us undeserved mercy, we offer our wounded and rejected hearts so that we may mend and extend mercy to those from whom we are estranged. Whatever has separated us cannot measure to the separation of a sinful people from a righteous God. Amen.

A Prayer of Reconciliation

Loving God, upon reflection, prayer, and counseling, we now know what brought us together as a unit is far more valuable than what separated us. Bring us together again as a family, in love and faithfulness. Bind us together again with chords that cannot be broken. Amen.

Tapping into My Superpower

MY PRAYER PETITION

_____

_____

_____

_____

_____

_____

_____

_____

_____

God is our Refuge

"Prayer helps us to hold our hope."

During a religious pilgrimage, young Jesus got separated from His early parents for what we deduce was a few hours. Although He was safe and "about His Father's business," Joseph and Mary were terrified. This is a natural emotion for any loving and responsible parent.

According to a *USA Today* report (Dec 2020), about 628 children were still missing due to the cruel family separation policy in place to deter immigrants and refugees from coming to the U.S. The policy has not been successful in its intent, but the impact will have repercussions for many generations. Psychologists have warned that the psychological trauma caused by the policy will be long lasting. Long before Joseph led Jesus and His mother Mary to Egypt to seek refuge from a murderous Herod the Great, families had been crossing borders in search of safety. They still do, to this day. God will judge harshly a regime that causes families to uproot themselves and run for safety. God will be harsh, but justified, in judging nations that turn away those who run toward them to find refuge, peace, and security.

A Prayer for Missing/Separated Immigrant Children

Elohim Machase, You are a refuge from all that makes us afraid, including storms, evil doers, and cruel regimes. We pray for the children who were torn from the loving arms of their parents. We pray that those still separated will be reunited with their families. We pray You heal all wounds caused by harmful experiences, both intentional and accidental. Amen.

A Prayer for Refugee Children

Jesus, You once had to flee a tyrannical ruler. Grant all refugee families, especially children, the opportunity to settle in peace and security. Amen.

Tapping into My Superpower

MY PRAYER PETITION

_____

_____

_____

_____

_____

_____

_____

_____

_____

_____

_____

_____

_____

JUSTICE: Concern for Oppressed Women

"Prayer is the strength of the weak, the comfort of the distressed, the empowerment of the oppressed, and hope of the forsaken."

Micah 6:8 reminds us, "He hath shewed thee, O man, what is good; and what doth the Lord require of thee, but to do justly, and to love mercy, and to walk humbly with thy God." YHWH desires us to have a different heart—one that fully loves God and loves our neighbors. Any effort or contribution that falls short of that is futile.

Justice emanates from love. Equal opportunity and equal treatment are both essential elements of social justice. When it comes to resources, social justice is concerned with ensuring fairness and equity for those who do not have the same access to it. One group that is often treated peripherally are women. For example, some Christian women are often in spaces where their voices are muted. Then, there is violence (physical, sexual, and verbal) against girls and women. Those who heed God's call to righteousness and justice realize that prayer and advocacy go hand in hand. To stand with survivors of violence, a call for congregational unity by encouraging women to speak out, is critical. Recognizing each woman's inherent dignity, we ask that the Church helps to create a safe place where people who have experienced violence can tell their stories. Genesis 1:26 specifies that everyone is made in the image of God. The world is held equally by and wholly in the hands of women. God's image is disfigured by all forms of abuse. Therefore, the assault is on God. Too long have the voices of women and girls remained unheard. No woman, anywhere, should ever be touched inappropriately. When a woman is enslaved anywhere, she is enslaved with all of us. We commend our sisters in Christ to bear each other's burdens.

A Prayer for Victims of Sex Trafficking

Father, we come boldly to Your throne, interceding for victims of sex trafficking— those who have been taken, kidnapped, and misplaced. May You deliver and make a way of escape for these women and children. May Your angels be dispatched to provide divine security and deliver them from their enemies. Amen.

A Prayer for Survivors of Rape

Gracious God, Maker and Ruler of heaven and earth, please pour out Your spirit upon survivors of rape. Let Your Holy Spirit flood the souls of those who are hurt and broken. Touch their bodies and spirits, heal their hearts, restore their minds to wholeness, and allow them to see themselves as whole and healed. Amen.

A Prayer for the Displaced (migration, fleeing violence)

God, You are merciful and You know all things. We pray for all the men, women, and children who are displaced, leaving their homelands in pursuit of a better life. We ask for strength as they are forced to depart from their homes to escape oppression, persecution, and violence; may they find a safe space to live in freedom and to experience peace. Amen.

A Prayer for Survivors of Incest

Jesus, we come to You and pray for survivors of incest. Please renew the minds of those who may be struggling, having experienced the trauma of incest as children. Remove the shame, guilt, and anger. Heal their hearts with faith, trust, and love. Surround them with trusted people who can provide Godly counsel, speak life into their spirits, and deliver them from self-blame and condemnation. May Your Spirit fill them with peace. Amen.

A Prayer for the Wrongfully Accused

Dear Lord, let the truth come out regarding those who are wrongfully accused, and let Your will be done. Provide deliverance to those who feel weary, worn, and hopeless. Strengthen their hearts today. Reveal Your plan and purpose for their lives. Help them find security and freedom in You. Amen.

A Prayer for Justice to Roll Down

Thank You for the breath of life. Breathe upon us, breath of God. Fill us with life anew. We confess our sins and failures. But even now, let justice roll down like waters in our nations and righteousness like an overflowing stream.

A Prayer for Judges

Spirit of the Living God, fall fresh on Your judges. Give them wisdom, knowledge, and understanding hearts to judge Your people so that they may discern between good and evil. Holy Spirit, led and guide judges into all truth; give them discernment to know the difference between guilty and innocent. May they reflect Your heart with compassion. Amen.

A Prayer for Help to Live Justly

Father, let us not seek to dismantle racism and injustice only through our demonstrations, but through our prayers, rhetoric, voting, economic practices, how we teach, how we share the gospel, the curricula we design, the types of prayers we pray, how we treat our black and brown neighbors, how we engage with students, how we do church, how we counsel, how we tell history, how we lead, how we preside, how we think, how we raise our children, and the values we adopt. For it matters to You that we reject what is evil and embrace what is good. It matters to You that we reject hate and embrace love...that we reject violence and embrace peace...that we reject oppression and embrace justice. It matters to You that we work towards justice, reconciliation, and righteousness. Amen.

Tapping into My Superpower
MY PRAYER PETITION

_____

_____

_____

_____

_____

_____

_____

_____

_____

_____

_____

_____

God's Grace and God's Government

"Prayer is ask-cess."

Christians are commanded to "submit... to the ruling authorities" (Romans 13:1) and to pray "for kings and everyone who are in authority, that we may live a quiet and peaceable life in all godliness and reverence" (Romans 13:2, I Timothy 2:2). These remarks are all the more stunning when we consider that Paul wrote them during the reigns of Nero and Caligula, two of history's deadliest tyrants. We must always endeavor to collaborate with the ruling authorities, as long as we can do so without denying Christ or sacrificing our faith. That does not imply that we will support all of their policies or agree with every single action they take. This is particularly true in a democratic society, where it is the responsibility of responsible citizens to scrutinize public officials with a critical eye. Christians, on the other hand, must promote biblical holiness in a hostile culture while also showing respect for its leaders.

What exactly do the verses above imply? This is all there is to it: God has complete control over human affairs; at the same time, He allows people to make their own decisions and follow their own paths. In other words, without God's permission, no one can become a king, emperor, governor, president, senator, assemblyman, or mayor. However, this does not imply that having political power is a sign of God's blessing. The long and short of it is that God is in charge at all times. We may not have faith in the government, but we must have faith in God. We may demonstrate such faith in normal circumstances by cooperating with the government, paying our taxes, participating in the system, and staying out of trouble. However, this does not imply that we should be blind. We must never lose sight of the fact that human rulers are subject to a greater force. It is predicated on God's absolute sovereignty. In the event that these two powers come into direct confrontation with one another, Christians must "obey God rather than men" (Acts 5:29).

A Prayer for God to Take Charge

Sovereign God, let Your will be done and Your kingdom come on earth. Take charge, Father, and watch over Your creation even when some decisions are made not with people in mind, but to boost egos and political favor. In the name of the Father, Son, and Holy Spirit.

A Prayer for Holy Boldness

Holy Father, when government policies are in opposition to biblical mandates, give us courage to insist on godliness and to make holy choices. In Jesus' name, amen.

A Prayer for Our Government

O Lord, You said that the Government is upon Your shoulders and that when the righteous rule, the people rejoice. Search the hearts of our leaders and raise up godly men and women to rule in the fear of the Lord. Grant them humility and wisdom to lead. Amen

Tapping into My Superpower

MY PRAYER PETITION

_____

_____

_____

_____

_____

_____

_____

_____

_____

_____

_____

_____

The Government is on His Shoulders

"Prayer is bowing to His Lordship."

"For unto us a child is born, and a son is given, and the government will be on his shoulders" (Isaiah 9:6). This verse from the 8th century prophet leads to the question: What are the benefits of having a godly administration? Everyone has heard about church shootings, school shootings, Las Vegas strip shootings, Chicago shootings, the terrorist incident in New York, and other global barbarities. The United States of America was founded on Christian principles...a foundation for prayer...a foundation for acknowledging God. It's no accident that these heinous crimes are taking place in America at the same time that God's Word is becoming extinct in our political realm.

Individuals are struggling to know and experience God, while our government is removing all traces of Christianity from the laws and legacy upon which our lives are based. The fast-approaching abolition of Christianity in America is affecting not only how people are starting to despise one another, but also how they are losing regard for human life itself. Although our government and popular media characters would like to believe that passing gun regulations and removing political officials will stop the violence and hatred, the grim reality is that our government will never be able to control the demented people who perpetrate these atrocities.

For the development of American society, we do not need to fix our government. Our government must correct the newly constructed "social standards" produced, which have led to the expulsion of Christianity. It's natural for people to hold different religious beliefs, and that's acceptable. Despite the atrocities committed against the First Nation and Africans and descendants of Africans, many decent colonists did hold to Christian values, and these have kept the country.

All of this is not to say that America is doomed or that we have lost our humanity. As long as faithful Christians continue to pray, we leave room for God to act. The government is on His shoulders. We're having a hard time, but the individuals on the other end of the spectrum keep us going. The reason we need God in government, today far more than we will ever need our government, is that our government will fail us. However, there is a hope that is far greater than faith in our government: faith that our God will not fail us.

A Prayer for Rulers

O God, today I present to You the world's rulers—kings, queens, presidents, and prime ministers—all of whom possess positions of great power. I pray that Your righteousness will reign in their hearts.

A Prayer for Godly Decision-Making

I'm quick to criticize. Please, Lord, assist me with first entering their predicament. I have the luxury of deferring judgment, of not committing myself, of sitting on the fence when it comes to most problems of state. Even when I have an opinion, it has little weight and is rarely acted upon. This is not the case with nation/state leadership. They must make decisions, even if they are lousy ones, to the extent that they truly lead. Give them wisdom to make good decisions. Amen.

A Prayer that Leaders Would Repent

We pray for and lift up every one of our leaders to You, asking that they look to You individually and collectively so that our countries can be governed according to Your plans and purposes. But, if we are to face Your wrath as a nation because we have broken Your laws and turned away from Your monuments, we pray that You would be gracious and that many of our leaders will cry out to You for forgiveness and help. This we beg for the sake of our Lord and Savior, Jesus Christ.

A Prayer for Salvation

Lord, I know that many—probably most— councilmen and councilwomen are unfamiliar with You and do not seek You. But You go out of Your way to find them! Save and deliver them and give them the courage to walk in the Light now that they've seen it. In Jesus' name, Amen.

A Prayer for a Turning Back to God

Father, we thank You for the countless gifts You have given on our country, blessings we do not deserve but You have bestowed on us in Your kindness and mercy. But, Father, we recognize that our country has lost its course and that our government is spiraling out of control, and we have no one else to turn to but You. We pray that You will look down on our country with compassion and mercy and that our leadership would be convinced of the need to return to You for wisdom to manage our nation in a way that honors Your name. Amen.

A Prayer for Integrity in Leadership

Holy Father, authority is properly managed, laws are legislated, and judgment is decreed by You, God of strength and might, wisdom and justice. Assist the President and other government leaders of the United States with Your wisdom and fortitude. May they always seek the paths of justice, mercy, and righteousness. Grant Your tremendous protection that would enable them to lead our country with honesty and integrity. We make our request in the name of Jesus Christ, our Lord.

A Prayer for Committee Members

Father in Heaven, allow committee members to observe the excellent deeds that people of faith are doing in their states and districts. Allow them to see what You are accomplishing through Your Church and the wonderful believers all around the country. Encourage them to support causes that honor You rather than their own political ambitions. Cut through the chaff of conventional politics and self-promotion. Allow them to hear Your words of dignity, sacrifice, and purity. We pray that the Holy Spirit will infuse our leaders with Your wisdom, understanding, counsel, might, and knowledge. Favor them, strengthen their faith, and equip them to achieve Your brilliance. Attract our leaders to You and help them understand and carry out Your purposes. In the name of Jesus, Amen.

A Prayer for Godly Counselors

Please put someone in the path of local, state, and national leaders who will give them scriptural, sound, and godly advice, for without it, their plans will go awry. Give them Your revelation about leadership and assist them in leading. Educate our leaders on the importance of keeping their hearts and motives pure. We pray that You will soften their hearts, making them receptive and obedient to Your will. Allow Your Name to be glorified in each of their lives. Father, we pray that You will raise up modern-day Davids, Solomons, Josephs, Nehemiahs, Deborahs, Ruths, and Esthers to serve in the political sector joyously and intentionally to assist rebuild and restore all nations. Amen.

A Prayer for Forgiveness for Politicians

Father, please forgive politicians for all sins, including jealously, disdain, pride, bitterness, criticism, lying, gossiping, hatred, grudges, revenge, and misappropriation of public monies. Forgive them when they participate in deceptive acts and oppressive practices, such as avoiding questioning, embellishing the facts, and failing to meet the necessities (e.g., food, housing, and jobs) of the people they serve. Forgive those politicians who ask You to forgive them when they refuse to forgive others for past transgressions. Please, Holy Spirit, remind all political leaders of people who need forgiveness from them and assist them in forgiving quickly. As for me, Holy Spirit, remind me of the people I need to forgive. Lord, I trust You to heal any unforgiveness-related scars in my soul. Help political leaders resist temptation and deliver them from the evil one, Holy Spirit. You, Lord God Almighty, who was, is, and will be, are Holy, Holy, Holy. You are the only one who is God. You are not subject to anyone, but You are subject to everything. Forever, the dominion, the power, and the glory are Yours. Amen, in Jesus' name.

Tapping into My Superpower

MY PRAYER PETITION

_____

_____

_____

_____

_____

_____

_____

_____

_____

_____

_____

_____

_____

Government and Grace

"When we pray, believe that He (God) has the whole world in His hands."

With divisive political views and apparently continuous debates about what constitutes "good governance" or "godly leaders," it can be difficult to understand what God thinks about government. It can be even more difficult for us to comprehend how Christians should act and think. The systems of this world are in a state of 'fallenness' because we are fallen people. Government, however, is not a novel way of organizing people, and God has a lot to say about world systems. We can find Bible verses about government and leaders throughout the Bible. These include:

For dominion belongs to the Lord and he rules over the nations. (Psalm 22:28)

Appoint judges and officials for each of your tribes in every town the Lord your God is giving you, and they shall judge the people fairly. Do not pervert justice or show partiality. Do not accept a bribe, for a bribe blinds the eyes of the wise and twists the words of the innocent. Follow justice and justice alone, so that you may live and possess the land the Lord your God is giving you. (Deuteronomy 16:18-20)

In the Lord's hand the king's heart is a stream of water that he channels toward all who please him. (Proverbs 21:1)

Praise be to the name of God for ever and ever; wisdom and power are his. He changes times and seasons; he deposes kings and raises up. (Daniel 2:20-21)

For to us a child is born, to us a son is given, and the government will be on his shoulders. And he will be called Wonderful Counselor, Mighty God, Everlasting Father, Prince of Peace. (Isaiah 9:6)

In every town the Lord your God gives you, appoint judges and officials for each of your tribes, and they shall judge the people equitably. Do not tamper with the justice system or exhibit favoritism. Accept no bribe, for a bribe blinds the wise and alters the words of the innocent. So that you may live and possess the land that the Lord your God is giving you, follow justice and justice alone.

God is the one who judges: he lowers one and raises another. (Psalm 75:7)

These and many other texts and teachings in the Bible concern governance and leaders. So, what is the Bible's take on government? For starters, God desires that we obey Him and the authorities. It is first necessary to recognize that God is the ultimate governance. God reigns supreme as the Creator of the cosmos, the One who created every person on the planet, and the One who has an ultimate plan. He is the One who makes the decisions and plots our course. He is the One who provides us our rules and directives. God is Sovereign and has the whole world in His hands. All we have to do now is follow Him.

However, God always puts people (select leaders) in positions to instruct the people. He talked to Joseph, and Joseph spared

God's people, the Israelites, from hunger (Genesis 47). Moses was called by God, and he led the Israelites out of Egypt and into the Promised Land (Exodus 13). Battles raged and towns were overturned as God spoke to monarchs.

Essentially, government's biblical mission is to serve as a guide, to lead and exercise authority over the people. While God is our Ultimate King, our earthly "kings" (rulers and systems) are to rule over us. Part of tapping into our superpower requires us to pray for leaders and systems that they may be subjected to God's Will and that God's Will *will* be done regardless of tyranny, despotism, liberalism, conservative or unjust policies and laws.

A Prayer for Our Government

Father, I lay our government's needs before You and ask that You bless our country by sending godly leaders. I exalt Jesus' name and declare Him to be the King of this land. In Jesus' name, amen.

A Prayer for Those in High Offices

Father, I pray that our Vice President, the members of the Cabinet, and the Chief Justice and associate Justices of the Supreme Court receive Your wisdom, act in accordance to that wisdom, and allow Your power to flow through them. Amen.

A Prayer for Government Officials

I pray for Your peace and direction for the members of the Senate and House of Representatives and for these men and women to act and lead according to Your Word. I pray for them to be united in justice for the sake of the nation because a house divided against itself cannot stand. I pray for Your protection over all of our law enforcement officers and military personnel. I pray for godly guidance and wisdom for judges all around the country. In Jesus' name, I ask that You and Your Kingdom of righteousness be manifested in the hearts of all those in positions of authority.

Tapping into My Superpower

MY PRAYER PETITION

_____

_____

_____

_____

_____

_____

_____

_____

_____

_____

_____

_____

Prayers and Politics

"Praying is political."

Because we live in politically divisive times, there has been a lot of talk about Christianity and politics: What is the Christian's role in politics? As Christians, if Jesus is our Teacher and Model, we must always, first and foremost, look to what He says about politics and governance.

Jesus stated that the most important commandment is to "Love the Lord your God with all your heart, soul, and mind" (Matthew 22:37), and that "all authority in heaven and on earth has been handed to me" (Matthew 28:18). However, everything on earth—things of the world—is subject to worldly authority. When asked if people were supposed to pay the imperial tax to Caesar, the land's then king, Jesus showed them the coin that was used as currency. "So give back to Caesar what is Caesar's, and to God what is God's," Jesus said, pointing to Caesar's image on the coin (Matthew 22:21).

When we consider these and other declarations and instances from Jesus' life, we can see that He consistently refers to the One Authority—God, the Father—as the true Ruler of the cosmos. However, when it comes to earthly things, they are less significant because our lives on this planet are only fleeting. As a result, while we are on Earth, we deduce that we must pay our taxes and obey the rules of the state as a matter of course. On earth, after all, God made it that way. These earthly things, however, are less significant when contrasted with the matters of the Kingdom of God.

The most significant truth is that we belong to God. Our true Ruler is God, and nothing should stand in the way of our relationship with our Lord.

A Prayer for the President

Our President, Father, bears a tremendous responsibility. President Biden's decisions have an impact on people not just in our country, but all throughout the world, and he needs Your help to lead. Lord, strengthen him. Give him grace and wisdom. In all situations, allow him to talk and behave with honesty and integrity. Give him a glimpse of how much You care for him and the world You've created. Attract him to You, Jesus, and draw him into a closer connection with You. Holy Spirit, anoint him. Speak to him both in the quiet and in the midst of the tumult. Make him a true servant leader by softening his heart. Surround him with powerful, knowledgeable, and spiritually mature individuals. Speak the truth to him in the voices of those he respects. Give him the wisdom to ignore those who urge him to pursue just personal power and glory. Allow him to understand that the victory can only be won with and through YOU. Our country and the planet are only complete because of Your power. Amen, in Jesus' name.

A Prayer for Congress

We pray for our members of Congress, both the Senate and the House of Representatives, in the name of the Lord. Bring them closer to You by revealing Yourself to them in their own unique way so that they can clearly hear Your voice. Speak to them about the importance of honesty, integrity, justice, and fairness. I pray that they will do the right things and remember why they ran for offices in the first place: to serve others, to correct wrongs, and to make the world a better place. Give each of them the courage to reach out to individuals on the other side of the aisle and collaborate. We humbly ask that You bind their hearts together in unexpected ways; let them exclaim, as King David did, "How good and delightful it is when God's people dwell in oneness!" You said, "What is impossible with man, is possible with God," and I believe You. Allow them to observe the good deeds that Your people of faith are doing in their states and districts. Allow them to see what You are accomplishing through Your Church and the wonderful believers all around the country. Encourage them to support causes that honor You rather than their own political ambitions. Amen.

Tapping into My Superpower

MY PRAYER PETITION

_____

_____

_____

_____

_____

_____

_____

_____

_____

_____

_____

_____

Obeying God/Obeying Government

"Prayer yields discernment so that the believer is equipped with knowledge that helps him/her navigate the murky waters of life."

"Whoever resists against the authorities is rebelling against what God has ordained," (Romans 13). Paul suggests that obeying God-established authorities is ordained by God. However, obeying the rules and leaders of this world should never come at the expense of obeying God's commandments. Every believer needs discernment to navigate with a spirit of godliness even in systems that are corrupt and unjust. If you're unsure whether to obey or honor government authorities, or if you're concerned about politics and how it might affect God's people, be assured that God is in charge. His Will always triumphs. Trust and obey to the best of your abilities.

Keep in mind that you are a citizen of Heaven. What does it imply that we have a Heavenly citizenship? A citizen is a person who is officially a citizen of a country and enjoys the country's privileges and protection. Citizens embrace the culture and habits of the country or kingdom they live in. We have the responsibility as residents of Heaven to demonstrate God's kingdom here on Earth. Jesus urges us to pray, "Your kingdom come, your will be done, on Earth as it is in Heaven" (Matthew 6:10).

A Prayer for State Leaders

You granted our forefathers with the foresight to partition our country into independent states, just as You rewarded Moses with wisdom to choose elders among the Israelites. You've given our governors and state legislatures the authority to enact laws and decrees that control our daily lives, keep us safe, and keep us protected from federal government overreach. I pray for our governors and state legislatures, in Jesus' name. Please grant them holy boldness, courage, and wisdom to guide their decisions, and may they always prioritize love. Surround them with godly men and women of integrity, and open their hearts to receive godly counsel. Bring persons and personnel with strong moral character and spiritual maturity to them. May they hear Your voice above all others, among the myriad of voices that scream out to them every day. Inspire and speak through our governors by the power of Your Holy Spirit as we look to them for assurance and guidance, especially in times of crisis.

A Prayer for a Godly Attitude towards Government

You are our True King, Almighty God. But please help us to understand that, just as in a family where the father and mother are to rule and be respected, so must we respect our government officials. You have a greater purpose, and it will be realized. Let us not do anything that would be counterproductive to Your goals. Help us to respect and appreciate those You have placed in positions of power on our planet. However, we must keep in mind that our time on this planet is limited. We are simply a mist that appears for a little time and then departs, as James 4 explains. The Kingdom of God, on the other hand, is eternal, and it is there where we have our actual citizenship. We pray in Your holy and precious name. Amen.

A Prayer for Local Leaders

I'm praying for our local leaders today, Jesus. We pray for our mayors, city councils, county commissioners, police chiefs, judges, and everyone else who serves our communities. For the enormous burdens they bear, strengthen them with wisdom and grace. May they lead with love in their teams and endeavors. As they work in the best interests of the people they are called to serve, keep their hearts clean and their eyes pointed on Your face. We are grateful to be in a democracy where we are free to openly pray for our elected officials. Amen, in Jesus' name.

A Thank You Prayer for Guiding our Government

Father, thank You for listening to my prayers that are in conformity with Your Will. In Jesus' Name, I receive the answers. Amen.

Tapping into My Superpower

MY PRAYER PETITION

_____

_____

_____

_____

_____

_____

_____

_____

For the Sick and Afflicted

"Our prayers are myopic. God's vision is majestic, so keep praying."

Who his own self bare our sins in his own body on the tree, that we, being dead to sins, should live unto righteousness: by whose stripes ye are healed. (1 Peter 2:24)

God's desire for you is that you will prosper and be in health even as your soul prospers (3 John 1:2). There is a connection between your soul and your health. Oftentimes, our internal struggles, conflicts, and misbeliefs manifest as bodily illnesses, such as migraine headaches, ulcers, high blood pressure, low blood pressure, and mental illnesses, such as depression. Other sicknesses, such as cancer, have biological pathways. But whatever the affliction, Jesus came to deliver us from all our sicknesses and diseases. Indeed, He came to destroy the works of the adversary (1John 3: 8).

The power of God is available for every impossible situation. You need not live in pain, discomfort, despair, and disbelief. Believe the report of the Lord over the report of doctors, your mind, or your body. Shut out the voices that want you to accept defeat. At the name of Jesus, every knee must bow and tongue confess that Jesus Christ is Lord. He is Lord over your sickness and disease. Believe that your portion is to live in health and do not become overwhelmed by affliction and fear. Do what is in your power to do: eat right, exercise, sleep well and get adequate rest, and practice self-care and spiritual renewal. After you have done all you can do, stand on God's promises for your life and confess His Word over your life and your situation. God wants to set you free so that you will enjoy His presence and be a witness of the power of God to heal, deliver, and set men free. Sickness was defeated at the cross, so walk in the health that was purchased for you on Calvary.

A Prayer for Release of Healing Anointing

I pray for a supernatural release of the anointing of God over your mind and your body now, in the name of Jesus. I release the anointing of healing over you and announce a speedy manifestation of health in you. Every spirit that is behind your infirmity, I command them to leave now, in the name of Jesus. Be healed, in Jesus' name. Amen.

A Prayer for Healing

Heavenly Father, I come to You because I know You are a healer. I pray, through the power of the Holy Ghost, that You touch me, from the crown of my head to the sole of my feet. I pray for healing in my body and in my mind. Oh God who created me, reconstruct everything in me that is not functioning in Your perfect will so that my body lines up with Your will for me. Deliver me from sickness and oppression so that I may fulfill my purpose and walk in my destiny all the days of my life. I pray that You will remove everything that cause sickness in my body and my mind and that Your grace and mercy will surround me all the days of my life. Amen.

Tapping into My Superpower

MY PRAYER PETITION

_____

_____

_____

_____

_____

_____

_____

_____

_____

_____

_____

_____

For Those in Hospice

"Prayers are healing waters that nourish in dry places."

Therefore, I say to you, take no thought for your life, what ye shall eat, or what ye shall drink, nor yet for your body, what ye shall put on. Is not life more than meat, and the body more than raiment? Behold the fowls of the air: for they sow not, neither do they reap, nor gather into barns; yet your heavenly Father feeds them. Are you not much better than they?
(Matthew 6: 25 – 27)

Sometimes, we find ourselves in places where it seems that death surrounds us and negative ideations intrude on our thoughts. You may even be in a place that causes you to doubt God's faithfulness. Do not give up. God has not forsaken you, neither has He abandoned you. The message in the passage of scripture above, from Matthew Chapter 6, is a message of hope that the Almighty God is aware of you and knows your situation. It is in such challenging times that we need to hear and meditate on the good news of God's loving kindness and tender mercies.

It is easy to praise God when times are good. The truth is, God is still God, irrespective of your circumstances. Habakkuk 3:17 -19 paints a picture of gloom. Here the prophet made a declaration: "*Although the fig tree shall not blossom, neither shall fruit be in the vines; the labor of olive shall fail, and the fields yield no meat; the flock shall be cut off from the fold, and there shall be no herd in the stalls: Yet I will rejoice in the Lord, I will joy in the God of my salvation, the Lord God is my strength.*" Can you still trust God when desolation is all around.? Can you rise up in hope as you trust in God's love for you, even when this love is hidden by the dark challenges of your situation? Our hope remains in the assurance that God has a plan for your life and His plan will never fail. It might be a season of testing but keep looking up; the season of breakthroughs will come. Offer a praise to God no matter where you find yourself and experience His presence even in your midnight hours. Declare that God is your strength.

A Prayer for Comfort

Holy Father, You are great and mighty, and there is none to compare to You. I pray for Your comfort and peace. I pray that You will set my spirit free to worship You in the beauty of holiness. Deliver me from evil and bring me out into a large place for Your name's sake. Amen.

A Prayer to Remain in God's Presence

Lord, when I am down and life's challenges seem overwhelming, help me to draw strength from You. I confess that at times I take my eyes off You and focus on my surrounding. Forgive my unbelief and restore my soul as I walk through this dark valley. I pray that I remain in Your presence to experience the joy and hope of knowing that I am precious in Your sight and Your Word for my life shall never fail. Thank You for Your love, and I ask that You anoint me with fresh oil so that my cup overflows. I pray that my mouth will be filled with Your praises in the good times, the in-between times, and the challenging times. I praise Your name because there is no God like You, and You have never lost a battle. Hallelujah and Amen

Tapping into My Superpower

MY PRAYER PETITION

_____

_____

_____

_____

_____

_____

_____

_____

_____

_____

_____

_____

For Those Struggling with Mental Wellness

"Prayer says, 'I can't but God can.'"

Many are the afflictions of the righteous: but the Lord delivers him/her out of them all (Psalm 34: 19)

No-one is immune from the stresses of life and the sudden challenges that arise and, at times, will seem unbearable. Even the strong becomes weary and experience negative mental health. God promises to give power to the faint and *"to them that has no might he increases strength"* (Isaiah 40:29). But what can you do while you wait on God? To manage mental stress, you need to reset and recharge as you draw close to God so that your soul will be refreshed. Your soul is the seat of your emotions and is connected to your thoughts (cognition and perception) and your brain (hormones). So, if you perceive that your situation is hopeless based on the evidence (you may have lost your job or have mountains of bills), your thoughts tend to be of gloom and doom ('I will be evicted' or 'I cannot pay my bills'). You may begin to experience feelings of anxiety and doubt, thus opening the door to depression or mood swings. But when you have an anchor, even when you falter, your faith rises to remind you that God is in control of your destiny.

A Prayer for Peace

My Lord and my God, I come to You today to receive Your strength because I am feeling low in spirit. I need Your help because I am unable to pull myself out of this affliction. Lord God, I need Your peace in my mind and in my thoughts. I place my trust in You because I know that You are my refuge and strength. Send Your word I pray and cause a shifting, a change in my situation and silence the voices in my environment that rise against Your will for my life. I pray this prayer in the name of Jesus. Amen

Tapping into My Superpower

MY PRAYER PETITION

_____

_____

_____

_____

_____

_____

_____

_____

_____

_____

_____

When Strong People Become Weak and Weary

"When the heart prays, God hears that, too."

David, a man after God's own heart, had bouts of depression. In Psalm 42:5, he cried out from the depths of his anguish, *"Why art thou cast down, O my soul? And why art thou disquieted in me? Hope thou in God: for I shall yet praise him for the help of his countenance."* This is a cry and a prayer. David proposed praising God, even when the soul is disquieted. During struggles with mental wellness, it is easy to spiral down into despair and hopelessness. In such instances, your strength may diminish. But God offers His strength, and your response should be to have hope in God, believing that He answers prayers, *casting all your cares upon him, for he cares for you* (1 Peter 5:7). Look back and remember that the God on the mountain is still the God in the valley and that it is in the valley (your low ebb), that your soul is restored.

A Prayer for Victory in Dark Places

By faith, Lord, I offer my praises to You because You are worthy of all the praise. As I praise You, saturate my soul so that I will come out of this dark place with joy and victory. Lead me through this valley and restore my soul because my hope is in You alone. Thank You for hearing my prayer. Amen.

A Prayer for Victory in Life

Lord of my weary days, I pray that Your grace will be sufficient as I cast my weaknesses on You because I know You care for me. Grant me the power to remain strong and the strength to live my life in victory. Amen.

Tapping into My Superpower

MY PRAYER PETITION

_____

_____

_____

_____

_____

_____

_____

_____

_____

_____

_____

_____

For Those Struggling with Addiction

"When our lips are silent, God hears the prayers of pain emanating from our hearts and the tears overflowing from our eyes."

My grace is sufficient for thee: for my strength is made perfect in weakness (2 Corinthian 12:9)

Sometimes, it seems that our lives may be stuck, and we cannot see a way out or the path forward is surrounded by darkness. You may be crying out to be set free from the addiction that you have been struggling with for years, or you are seeking a balm to dull your pains. God did not create you to search out and become consumed with the fires of addiction. You may feel bound and in chains because you have tried, on your own, to be free of your addiction, but your efforts have fallen short. God is your help, and He will never leave you nor forsake you. He also will send you the help that you need to be victorious over addictions. Discussions surrounding seeking help outside the church are more common now than in times past. But there is still a stigma associated with seeking help from professionals. You need to recognize that in some instances, prayer alone will not work, but you can win with the help of trained professionals who will guide you through the process of being free from addiction.

Additionally, your spiritual growth will form a buffer against addictions, as the more you grow in the Word and grace of God, the less the addicted mentality (thoughts and behaviors associated with addictions) will manifest. You are never alone, but you may need to surround yourself with a mentor or tutor that will hold you accountable in your walk of faith. Remember, it is the grace of God that keeps us all. In your walk to become totally free from the chains of addiction, do not berate yourself if you stumble and fall. Get back up again and hold on to your faith in the God who can deliver and set you free from bondage. Jesus can break every chain *and whom the Son sets free is free indeed* (John 8:36).

A Prayer for Victory over Distress

I pray that the hand of God will heal me from addiction and destroy the hold of addiction from my life. Give me victory over my distress. I pray that the fire of the Holy Ghost will fall upon me and that I will walk in faith to victory over everything that concerns me. Amen.

A Prayer for Deliverance from Addiction

Heavenly Father, I know when I am weak, You remain strong, for there is no searching out of Your understanding and Your grace is sufficient for me. Hide me under Your wings and cause me to walk in my purpose. I pray that You will heal, deliver, and set me free from every form of addiction, and every persistent problem that rises up against me. Send Your word and set me free. Manifest Your glory in my tastes and appetites so that the desires for the things that cause addiction will not manifest in me. Help me to make restitution to all those that I have wronged during my state of addiction and to set an example of Your grace and mercy that redeems. Amen.

Tapping into My Superpower

MY PRAYER PETITION

_____

_____

_____

_____

_____

_____

_____

_____

_____

_____

_____

_____

_____

For Those Struggling with Suicidal Ideations

"Prayer brings our will into alignment with God's Will."

The thief comes to steal, to kill, and to destroy. I am come that they might have life, and they might have it more abundantly (John 10:10)

The Lord wants you to live an abundant life. His desire is that we will live and not die before our time. There are times in our lives when we get weary and feel hopeless. When you get to the point of hopelessness and the belief that there will be no change in your situation and that the best recourse is to end your life, pause and ask yourself, "Does my life have value?" The answer is, "Yes." You are not your own. You were bought with a price (1 Corinthians 6: 19-20). You are precious in the sight of God. Not only are you precious, but you were created and fashioned in the image of God. Most of the time when you have a suicidal thought, you are looking inward and concluding that the world will be better off without you and that, through dying, the situation you face will cease from evoking pain and stress. Some people may believe that they are sick unto death, so it is best to end their lives rather than prolong the pain and suffering. However, as long as there is life, there is hope. Since God wants you to live, then suicide is contrary to the Will of God. We wrestle against spiritual wickedness in high places (Ephesians 6:12). So, do not collaborate with the enemy of your soul that wants you to die before your time. I hope that the Spirit of God who lives in you will rise up when self-injurious beliefs and behaviors intrude in your thoughts and that the Spirit of God will cause you to declare, *"I shall not die but live and declare the works of the Lord" (*Psalm 118:17*)*. The spirit of death is real, but I pray that you will not abandon your mission and purpose. Meditate on God's promise that tells you that He knows the thoughts that He thinks toward you, thoughts of peace, and not of evil, to give you an expected end (Jeremiah 29: 11). God's plan is that you will know His will for you and embrace that you are the beloved child of the Highest. God wants to bless you and make you a blessing to others. So live.

A Prayer for Deliverance in Mind and Body

My God and my King, I bow before Your throne to praise Your name. I pray that my desires will line up with Your perfect will for my life. I confess that I have allowed fear and anxiety to overwhelm me at times. I pray when I am afraid and want to give up, You will show Yourself strong and mighty and that Your power will manifest in my thoughts and mind. Deliver me from suicidal thoughts and cause my mind to remain sound as You transform me into the person You want me to be. I pray that I will live to declare Your mighty works and walk in my purpose and fulfill my destiny. In the name of Jesus, Amen.

A Prayer against the Spirit of Death

I rebuke the spirit of untimely death from over my life, now, in the name of Jesus. I pray, in the power of the Holy Ghost, that I cast off the cloak of depression and suicide and take captive every thought to the obedience of Christ. I pray God will do a new thing in me and that as I wait upon the Lord, my strength shall be renewed, in the name of Jesus. Amen.

Tapping into My Superpower

MY PRAYER PETITION

_____

_____

_____

_____

_____

_____

_____

_____

_____

For Supernatural Deliverance

"You will never get a busy signal or a recorded message when you call on God through prayer."

God is able to deliver. That is our confidence as children of God. It does not matter if your need is for a spiritual deliverance, financial deliverance, psychological deliverance, or physical deliverance; God is able. We can focus on our difficult situations, or we can focus on the majesty of our God. The question was asked in Jeremiah 32:27, *"Behold, I am the Lord, the God of all flesh: Is there anything too hard for me?"* The answer to that question is a resounding, "Nothing is too difficult for God." The Bible is replete with testimonies of the faithful God delivering His servants and the people of Israel time and time again. You may have experienced the hand of God as He has blessed you and intervened for you in miraculous ways. In Exodus 17, we also read that God intervened in the battle and guaranteed victory for His people. After the victory, Moses wrote that God is Jehovah Nissi or Yahweh-Nissi: The Lord is my Banner. May you encounter Jehovah Nissi today. May you shout for joy as you encounter a life-changing, destiny changing experience with Almighty God. Jesus died so that you will not be bound but will be delivered from the chains of bondage. Additionally, Jesus conquered death, hell, and the grave so that you will attain the victory. Victory means that you have gone through a battle. You are destined to win and the Greater One that resides in you will deliver you from all bondage. When God turns your captivity around, your tests shall be your testimonies. So, activate your faith; activate your superpower within, and believe the Word of God for you and your situation.

A Prayer for my Destiny

Heavenly Father, You are the God whose Word commands my destiny. I believe that You are with me and that You watch over me. Speak life to my destiny and anoint me with fresh oil until I am fully assured that because I trust in You, I am like Mount Zion, which cannot be moved but stands forever. Destroy the plan of the enemy for my life. Use the things that were sent as burdens and make them steppingstones to the blessings You have in store for me. Hallelujah and amen.

A Prayer for Breakthrough

Lord God, You are the God of my breakthrough, the God of my deliverance. You are God all by Yourself. You are always on time. Cause me to hold on until my change comes, knowing that it is not over until You say so. Thank You for delivering me from all afflictions and giving me victory on every level. I declare that it is well because I trust in You. I pray in the name of Jesus, Amen.

Tapping into My Superpower

MY PRAYER PETITION

_____

_____

_____

_____

_____

_____

_____

_____

_____

_____

_____

What's Love Got to Do with It?

"When we pray, we tap into God's love."

"But the fruit of the Spirit is love"
(Galatians 5:22-23)

The *Amplified Bible* states that the Fruits of the Spirit are the result of His Presence within us. Love is the first fruit listed. God reminds us that to bear fruit starts in Him. Jesus epitomizes Love when He sacrificed Himself on the cross to redeem us from sin. Christians are enjoined to follow Christ with unselfish concern for others. When we walk in love, we demonstrate Jesus to a world that has become cold and uncaring. To love, we must know the God who is Love. Only then can we care for others to the degree that we place their concerns as the priority over our own. It starts, first, with loving Christ, then accepting yourself as a child of God, and then seeing others in the light of God's love.

A Prayer to Receive God's Love

Holy Spirit, I ask that You take my prayers to my Heavenly Father, as I recognize that He gave His Only Son to demonstrate His love for me. I pray that you prepare my heart to receive and manifest His great love. I pray that from this point onward, His love will permeate in all areas of my life. Amen.

A Prayer to Manifest His love to Others

Heavenly Father, I have fallen short so often, especially in forgiving others who have hurt and used me. Please forgive me. I pray that You will restore me so that my heart will experience the love I once had for You and that I will show Your love to those around me. Amen.

Tapping into My Superpower

MY PRAYER PETITION

_____

_____

_____

_____

_____

_____

_____

_____

_____

_____

_____

_____

Gentleness and Kindness

"It's important to pray for the fruit of the spirit."

We are prone to be encouraged by a kind act or an act of gentleness towards us. That feeling we experience should be bottled up and remembered whenever we are tempted to repay tit-for-tat or evil-for-evil. As Children of God, we ought to follow the Lord's example: though He was reviled, He did not retaliate but responded with love. A soft, gentle answer is capable of diffusing any wrath. You have the ability to bless or curse with your words. You have the ability to show kindness in face of rejection or to hate. Tap into your superpower and show kindness and gentleness, and let the Lord take care of the rest.

Prayer for Gentleness and Kindness

Father Lord, my desire is to be more like You. Wash me thoroughly in Your Blood until I become more like Your Son, Jesus Christ. I confess that I do not always show kindness or gentleness nor have I desired to do so when faced with brutish individuals. But help me, empower me, and grant me the grace to want to show kindness and gentleness in words and deeds. Amen.

Prayer to Manifest Gentleness & Kindness

Loving God, I desire to live a life worthy of the name of Jesus and to reflect godly character in all my ways. Help me to make every effort to keep the oneness of the Spirit in the bond of peace by showing Your kindness to those I encounter. Help me to be kind and considerate to the needs of others. Amen.

Tapping into My Superpower

MY PRAYER PETITION

_____

_____

_____

_____

_____

_____

_____

_____

_____

_____

_____

_____

A Benevolent and Bountiful God

"The Fact that God would condescend to listen to our prayers is a sign of His goodness."

Most times, when we think of goodness, we think of blessings that chase after us, with mercy. But goodness is an extension of God, for the Lord is good (Psalm 100:5). Goodness is the state or quality we possess that is derived from God. The goodness of God is within us, and the more we yield to His presence within us, the more likely we are to show forth His goodness. When faced with a choice between good and evil, choose good and let goodness be the normal conduct of the children of God. Goodness is an action that should be practiced from the heart. If your heart is right before God and men, then showing goodness is the outward expression of a pure heart.

Prayer for Goodness

Heavenly Father, I know you as the Good Father. I need to be more like You in all my ways. In righteousness, anoint me afresh so that my desires align with Your Perfect Will for my life. As I expect to receive of Your goodness, let me do for others as I would like them to do for me. Amen.

Prayer to Manifest Goodness

Heavenly Father, teach me how to show Your goodness in a world that has grown cold and uncaring. In my environment, let me be Your light to show Your goodness so that others will be drawn to the God in me. Amen.

Tapping into My Superpower

MY PRAYER PETITION

_____

_____

_____

_____

_____

_____

_____

_____

_____

_____

_____

_____

A Divine Approach for Dealing with Disappointment

"If prayer for you means praying for 'my will be done,' then there is no need to pray."

To deal with disappointment, we need to change our perspectives. We need to see situations from a divine perspective. Realize that Jesus never said we wouldn't encounter problems but that we should take heart amidst it all, since He has overcome this world (John 16:33): *"I have told you these things so that in me you may have peace. In this world you will have tribulation but if you abide in me, you will have peace."*

You are right where you are supposed to be for now, and as disappointed as you are, you are not going to be plucked out of that situation until your assignment has been completed. In dealing with disappointment, you should trust that God may be shielding you from something that would cause you great harm if you were to be given what you desire; trust that you may not be ready for the thing that you desperately desire and your immaturity would cause you to blow the blessing; trust that God is prepping you for your next level. God is building faith muscles, fine-tuning your character, strengthening your resolve in preparation for the next assignment and blessing. Trust God because as a loving Father, He knows what's best for us. Romans 8:28 assures us that, "God will work all things for good for those who love God and are called according to God's purpose." Trust God and pray for His Will, not your own, to be done in your life.

A Nevertheless Prayer

Father, there have been times we have been disappointed, and it has led to emotions that the enemy has used to ensnare us and turn our hearts away from You. Forgive us for the times when we have not brought our disappointments to You. In all situations, You know what's best for us; You know how You are molding and shaping and stretching and strengthening us. You know exactly how You are preparing us for our assignments and purpose. May Your highest and fullest potential for our lives be realized. Give us grace to continue to bring everything to You in prayer and grace to continue to wait on You, trust in You, and hope in You. Overall, Thy will be done in our lives. In Jesus' name, amen.

A Prayer to Remain in God's Will Despite Disappointment

Holy Father, if I am walking opposite of Your divine agenda, please reverse my course. In Jesus' name, Amen.

A Prayer to be Filled with the Fruit of the Spirit

My Lord and my God, please bless me with the Fruit of the Spirit and help me to wait and hope in You. Amen.

Tapping into My Superpower

MY PRAYER PETITION

_____

_____

_____

_____

_____

_____

_____

_____

Dealing with Discontent

**"Prayer is the soul's desire to seek
contentment in God."**

The Scriptures remind us, "To be anxious
for nothing but by prayer and supplication,
make your request be made known unto God
and the peace of God will keep your heart
and mind in Christ Jesus" (Philippians 4:6-
8). There are many reasons for discontent
(i.e., failing health, poor marriage, job loss,
career stagnation, singleness and loneliness,
rebellious children, loss of a spouse or loved
one, meager finances). Discontent is rooted
in the fact that we have certain expectations
for our lives that don't come to fruition. Ask
yourself: "Are my expectations, God's
expectations for my life?" The Holy Spirit
will give you the answer. If it's no, then
your prayer should be, "God reverse my
course and help me to walk in alignment
with Kingdom agenda." If you are desiring
something that hasn't materialized, ask God
to give you patience to wait in and for His
timing. In the fullness of time, He will

supply every need. In the between-time, you should be asking for God's peace and joy that will replace any spirits of bitterness, brokenness, anger, jealousy, rivalry, self-hate, and frustration.

<u>A Prayer to Refocus</u>

God, my desires and expectations may be too carnal. Perhaps, I am pursuing the world's idea of success instead of Yours. If that's the case redirect my footsteps and my focus. In Jesus' name, Amen.

Tapping into My Superpower

MY PRAYER PETITION

_____

_____

_____

_____

_____

_____

You Can Trust God

"Prayer is reliance on God. People don't pray to someone they can't rely on."

Trust implies confidence and confidence implies a healthy relationship. We don't have a relationship with people we don't trust. Trust is the cornerstone of a healthy relationship. It's the oxygen of a relationship. Without it, relationships don't last. For those who know God as Lord and Savior, there are benefits to trusting God. When we trust God, we can let our guard down and lean on God. We don't have to be self-reliant. We can be God-reliant.

Provers 3:5-6 says, "Trust in God with all your heart, and lean not on your own understanding. In all your ways acknowledge Him and he will direct your paths." The writer, Solomon, a man of wisdom, encourages us to put all our trust in God and commit all our ways to God, not just some ways but all ways, *always*. When I was an interim pastor at a local church, one of the deacons used to ask, "How much is All?" All means *all*. Trusting God doesn't imply we are logic-deficient, but we recognize the value of wisdom as we put trust in the Omniscient Creator of the universe who knows the future. Nothing can take God by surprise. Thus, we can look to God for help and hope. We can rely on His Word and wisdom, His love, and His promises and protection. The fact is that if we are walking with God, we don't always need to know where we are going because He will never lead us astray.

A Prayer for Continued Direction

God, as we lean on You, please never remove Your shoulder; please never withdraw You hand.

<u>A Prayer to Learn to Trust</u>

Help us, Father, to grow and develop trust in You. Help us to realize that You are the Author and Finisher of our faith, the Designer of the universe, the All-knowing and seeing One who is really in control of it all. Not only are You Sovereign, You have our best interests at heart.

Tapping into My Superpower

MY PRAYER PETITION

_____

_____

_____

_____

_____

_____

_____

_____

Everyday Prayers for People and Situations

"There are no perfect prayers, only a perfect God."

A Prayer for Reconciliation

Father God, our Ultimate Reality, the Source of all truth, the God of love, the God who created the nations, thank You for being an ever-present help in trouble. Thank You for the brave voices crying out for justice all over this nation. Like the blood of Abel that cried out to You from the ground, let the blood of the unjustly slain by police brutality come up to You. Help us embrace the truth that we are our brothers' and sisters' keeper. Strengthen the feet of many who through their protests raise awareness about racism and injustice.

Dismantle this evil virus. Send this demonic scourge back to the pit of hell. When we protest against injustice, let those protests be peaceful and impactful Keep bitterness from poisoning our hearts. Let order prevail. Keep safe men and women who bravely walk the streets for justice. Put a hedge of protection around them all. You are merciful. May it be said of this nation that, truly, here every creed and race finds an equal place. Show us, God, how to do justly, love mercy, and walk humbly with our God.

Heal the relationship between ethnic groups. Deliver us from a spirit of superiority. Give us a spirit of humility. Help us to turn the sword of anger into ploughshares that reap a harvest of reconciliation. Help us to embrace the truth that we are all Your creation. Help us to see each other's humanity. All lives can't matter until all people are treated with dignity and all individuals are judge according to the content of their characters and not the color of their skins. Help us to acknowledge, confess, and repent for the sins of our pasts. Forgive us our sins. Help us to work together to dismantle racism and undo injustice. Help us to work together to do what is right and just.

A Prayer for the Police

Father, thank You for blessing us with men and women who serve faithfully. Protect policemen and women who serve faithfully and serve well. Every day, at the end of their shifts, return every police officer home safely to their families. Deliver them from the assault and vindictiveness of villains. In Your goodness, safeguard them from all dangers, seen and unseen. In Jesus' name, Amen.

A Prayer for Police Reform

Let there be reforms in police academies and stations all over the nation. We pray for anti-racism training, cultural sensitivity training, and customer service training on how to police. In Jesus' name, Amen.

A Prayer for Wisdom

Father, give the police wisdom and discernment for when to use their weapons. May lives not be needlessly lost because of inappropriate use of weapons or restraining tactics. In Jesus' name, Amen.

A Prayer for Courage

Give policemen and women courage to perform their jobs with integrity. Amen.

A Prayer for Soldiers

For soldiers in combat, we pray that, in Your mercy, You will protect them, O Holy Father.

A Prayer for Nurses and Doctors

Watch over our nurses and doctors as they care for the sick and afflicted. At the end of their tours of duty, return them safely home to their loved ones and grant them special blessings. Amen.

A Prayer for Essential Workers

Lord who sets us in place and holds our futures, You have prepared special people to care for those in need. As they care for others, may their needs be met in You. Amen.

A Prayer for Teachers

God, You are wisdom, and You encourage us to ask You for wisdom in our daily lives.

Bless those who impart knowledge and grant them grace to persevere even when they feel discouraged. Amen.

Prayer for Joy

Father, I am confident that You formed and fashioned me from my mother's womb and that You know the thoughts that You think towards me. This confidence renews my hope when things are dark around me. I pray that I will be filled with Your joy so that my strength shall be restored and I continue to rejoice in You always. Amen.

Prayer to Manifest Peace

Father Lord, You are God. I come to You in the name of Your son, Jesus Christ. I acknowledge that I need You every hour. You have blessed me in abundance and have always deliver me from trouble and distress. Yet, I am prone to doubts and despair when the fires of life rage. Help me to not only experience Your peace, but to bring Your peace in every trying situations and circumstances. Amen.

Prayer for Patience

Heavenly Father, I know that Your grace is sufficient for me, but I get wearied in doing well and need Your Spirit to help me to accept Your will for my life. Cause me to wait patiently for You so that my strength shall be renewed like the eagle and that I may mount up above the cares of this life. Amen.

Prayer for Self-Control

Lord, let me do all things in moderation, and let me control my thoughts, words, and deeds for Your glory and honor. When I fail, help me to get up and start afresh in You, knowing that You have delivered me from the works of the flesh and that there is no condemnation in You. Amen.

Prayer for Meekness

Holy Father, let my spirit yield to you, so that you will delight to call me your own. I pray for a spirit that is truly meek and lowly and will remain resolute to practice this virtue in all contexts. Amen.

Tapping into My Superpower

MY PRAYER PETITION

_____

_____

_____

_____

_____

_____

_____

_____

_____

_____

_____

_____

Lamentations

"Since we have permission to 'cast our cares before God,' we have permission to lament."

When life overwhelms us and the storms of life assail, God's behavior remains consistent. He is still "our refuge and strength, a very present help in trouble" (Psalm 46:1).

A Prayer for Peace in the Midst of Turmoil

God of our weary years, God of our silent tears, God who has brought us this far along the way, Eternal One, who through Your prophets foretold a day when swords will be beaten into plowshares and who in Jesus Christ made peace through the blood of the cross, pour out Your Spirit on all people everywhere so that we may be delivered from hate, hostility, and self-seeking, and find our peace in Your Will. In Your mercy, make us instruments of Your peace so that

Your Name may be hallowed, Your Kingdom come, and Your Will be done on earth as it is in Heaven, through Jesus Christ, our Lord.

God of Abraham, Isaac, and Jacob; God of Esther, Ruth, and Naomi; God of Sojourner Truth, Harriet Tubman, and Frederick Douglass; God of Martin, Malcolm, and Rosa; God of Corrie Ten Boom; God of God who has washed us in the blood of the Lamb; God who has reconciled us in Your love; God who has led us with a strong arm and stretched out hand, continue to guide us through this turmoil, we pray.

A Lament for the Oppressed

Lord, help. There is crying in the land—not cries of joy but cries of gall from now-barren mothers.

Lord, help. There is moaning in the land—moaning carried by gusts of wind from the labor pains of injustice.

*Lord, help. There is trauma in the land—
trauma flowing from the deep memory wells
of generational abuse.*

*Lord, help. There is famine in the land—not
a lack of bread but of justice.*

*Lord, help. There is drought in the land—
not a drought of water but of justice.*

*Lord, help. There are silvery shouts in the
land as injustice saunters through burning
streets dressed like a queen in Babylon.*

*Clutching hearts,
Clutching heads,
Flowing rivers for eyes,
Trembling hands wrapped around dead
bodies,
Standing at gaping graves.*

*Lord, help. Does it matter to You that people
are hurting in this land?
Motherless
Fatherless
Widows*

*Lord, help. There is wailing in the land.
The ground still opens its mouth to receive
brothers' blood.*

The ground still opens its mouth to receive fathers' blood.
The ground still opens its mouth to receive the blood of sons and daughters.

Lord, help. Anguish, as wormwood, crawls through the land.

Lord of justice and righteousness, help. Make haste to heal the land.

A lament for black lives:
Remember, O Lord, what has come upon Your people, human beings created in Your image and likeness: Trayvon Martin, Tamir Rice, Michael Brown, Eric Garner, Philando Castile, Breonna Taylor, George Floyd, Sandra Bland, Rayshard Brooks, Elijah McClain, Jacob Blake.

Consider and behold our reproach. Our inheritance is turned to strangers, our houses to aliens. We are orphans and fatherless.
Our mothers are as widows.
Our fathers are childless.
Our sisters have lost brothers.
Our brothers have lost mothers and sisters.

We have been subjected to hate and oppression. We have been oppressed and afflicted. Our necks are under persecution. We labor for justice and inclusion and equity and equality and have no rest.

Our forefathers were brought to a nation that despised them, used their bodies for labor, and we have inherited the stigma of their reproach.

We are counted as pariahs, subjected to systemic oppression in housing, health, education, and banking, in law...

We got our bread with the peril of our lives under the burning eyes of Jim Crow and Jane Crow. Our skin is black like an oven because of the terrible famine of injustice.

They ravished our mothers in the cotton fields, homes, and across plantations.
Our sisters were subjected to scorn and ridicule.
Babies were plucked from the breast and sold.
Mothers wailing
Milk dripping from weeping breasts.

Cages built to capture freed slaves,

Counted as vagrants
Freed from plantations with nothing to feed
on
Millions illiterate
40 acres and a mule some got
Then, the "Thou shalt nots" of Jim Crow.

Vilified and terrorized by
Kind Kristian Kongregations
As wanderers, we are in the land.

Remember us, O Lord.
Our lives matter.

Our men were the strange fruit hanging
from trees. Black face did not honor the
faces of our elders. They took the young men
to grind, took them as studs.
Husbands were separated from wives.
Children from parents.
Masters bedded the wives of men who were
allowed to jump the broom.

Remember us, O Lord.
Our lives matter.

Have mercy on us.
Have mercy on the generations after us.

The joy of our heart is ceased.

Our dance is turned into mourning.
The crown is fallen from our head:
Woe unto us.
Our young men are subjected even now to
violence. A blue warrant of death has been
issued on our lives.

For this our heart is faint.
For this our soul is weary.
For these things our eyes are dim.

Thou, O Lord, who remains forever, Your
throne is from generation to generation.
Why have You forgotten us?
Why have You forsaken us for so long?
Turn Thou us unto Thee, O Lord, and we
shall be turned; renew our days and bring
glory to our years.

We lament for the sins we committed against
You, our God.
Forgive our sins.
Reconcile us to You.
Do not utterly reject us.
Do not be very angry against us.
Remember Cushite who is stretching her
hands to You.

You are the faith of our foremothers: Sarah,
Hagar, Rachel, Leah, Ruth, Naomi, Esther,

Harriet, Fannie Lou, Sojourner Truth,
Phyllis Wheatley.

You are the hope of the nations.
You are the wellspring of life.
No one who turns to You shall be rejected.

God of our weary years and our loud tears.
You have brought us this far.
Remember us, even now, O Lord.
Let justice roll down like waters.
Let righteousness flow like a stream.
Make haste to deliver us,
And we will forever praise You.
Bless us, O Lord for our lives matter.

A Lament for All Lives

Since all lives matter to You, help us to
honor all lives. Deliver us from a haughty,
demeaning, and condemning attitude that
causes us to despise and mistreat each
other. Let us never seek to justify oppression
of others who may be different from us. Help
us to see the image of God in all humanity.
Holy Father, help us to treat each other with
dignity, love, and respect. In Jesus' name.

Tapping into My Superpower

MY PRAYER PETITION

_____

_____

_____

_____

_____

_____

_____

_____

_____

_____

_____

_____

_____

One Minute Prayers

For Revival

The name of the Lord be exalted so that we will be revived, revitalized, and refreshed by Your glory. The fire of the Holy Spirit ignite our hearts with love for God and a passion to serve Him with all our hearts, souls, and minds. Amen.

For the Hungry

As individuals, we will not pass by those who are hungry but be the ones who provide their daily food. Nations who have plenty compassionately provide for nations in famine.

For Sanctification

Father, sanctify us by Your truth. Your Word is Truth. Amen.

A Prayer for Peace in the Church

May peace prevail in the body of Christ.

Against Night Terrors

No evil befalls us nor comes near our dwelling place.

Against Wickedness

The wicked will cease from troubling, and the weary will find rest from violence.

For Protection

God will be our refuge and our fortress and will deliver us and honor us.

On Being a Good Neighbor

Deliver us from bitterness and unforgiveness. Teach us how to truly be a good neighbor.

For the Land

Have mercy on us, loving Father.
Heal our nation.
Heal our land.
In Jesus' name, amen.

For Obedience

Father, in all things, teach us to obey You. Amen.

For the Lost

May the spiritually lost come to know Jesus as Savior.

For Healthy Marriages

May spouses love, respect, and revere each other.

For Financial Healing

Deliver from financial hardship and slavery to debt.

For Effective Stewardship

May we be wise stewards of the resources and blessings provided by God.

For Generational Blessings

May the curse of poverty be destroyed and those who have been poor have more than enough.

For Wars to Cease

God raise up government leaders who will be advocates for peace and justice.

For the Lonely

Relieve them of their loneliness.

For the Grieving

May those in mourning know Your comfort.

For the Unsaved

May those in bondage to strongholds experience deliverance through the power of the Holy Spirit.

For the Church

The Church will return to its first love and the Holy Spirit will rule in our affairs.

For the Aging

May they still bring forth fruit in old age

For Our Youth

The glory of the Lord will rise upon them

For Tyrants

May their hearts of stone be removed and may You create in them clean hearts and pure minds. Renew them with the right spirit.

For Creativity

May we be empowered with ideas for new businesses or initiatives.

For Business Investors

Send us the right investors and business partners who will not cheat us, sabotage us, or steal our ideas.

For the Right Employees

May we use wisdom and discernment in choosing the right employees for the right positions.

For the Poor

May You give them creative and innovative ideas that will help them advance in life.

For the Rich

May you show them the ways they can serve You through blessing others.

For the Imprisoned

Liberate them from mental slavery.

For those Wrongfully Imprisoned

May they receive justice and liberation.

For the Depressed

May the depressed be healed and re-discover life's joy.

For the Marginalized

May their needs will be supplied.

For Debt Elimination

May there be better stewardship of finances.

For Better Stewardship of Relationships

May we honor our friends and treat them with kindness.

For Those Mourning

May you comfort them and may they find joy in Your presence.

For Orphans

God will provide parent-figures in their lives, people who will be sources of support, inspiration, and encouragement.

For Those who have had Miscarriages

Father, would You please comfort those who have had miscarriages. Heal the pain, guilt, blame, and sense of hurt and bitterness that comes with loss of a child. And in the fullness of time, bless that woman, that couple, to be fruitful and bring to full term the healthy child/children they are longing for.

For Those Struggling with their Sexuality

God will help them and keep them from being bullied and ostracized.

For Immigrants

May they have a better life and become healthy, contributing citizens of the nations in which they are seeking residency.

For Police Brutality to Cease

May the police not physically abuse people in their custody but treat everyone with dignity.

For Police Reform

May positive, healthy reform that helps police to effectively handle people be instituted across the nation.

For the Safety of Police Officers

May policemen and women who face many hazards every day be kept safe. May they be protected from the hurt and harm of criminals, terrorists, and gang shoot-outs. Even as they walk through the valley of the shadow of death, we pray for God's watchful eyes to be over them.

For those Caring for the Sick

May they receive strength when they are weary and protection from sicknesses and diseases as they care for the helpless, the weak, and the hurting.

For Leaders

Holy Father, strengthen men and women to be good leaders, with humility, empathy, creativity, and character. Amen.

For Vision

Bless leaders with a God-given vision that will empower people to reach their highest and fullest potentials.

For the Ability to Face and Resolve Conflict

Give us the tenacity, insight, and peace-making ability to face and resolve conflicts, to dispel bitterness, anger, and strife, and lead to repentance, forgiveness, and reconciliation.

For Healing of the Nations

May righteousness abound because righteousness exalts a nation but sin is a reproach to people. Blessed is the nation whose God is the Lord.

For Those Traumatized by Sexual Abuse

May they find justice. May they be healed.

For Victims of Domestic Violence

May they be divinely protected from the hands of their abusers and provided the resources they need to live healthy lives.

For the Apathetic

May they be delivered from apathy. Give them new vigor and a purpose.

For the Apostate

May they be transformed by the renewing of their minds.

For Humility

Keep us humble. You say if we humble ourselves, You will exalt us.

For Ministry Help

God will keep calling men and women to serve.

For the Mission of the Church

God will keep us committed to discipleship.

For the Mind of Christ

May Christians everywhere have the mind of Christ.

For Good to Prevail

May wickedness in high places be eradicated and systemic strongholds be dismantled.

For the Wicked

The wicked will cease from troubling, and their counsel will be covered in confusion.

For Hope

May hope come to many who come to Christ.

For God's Will

May we yield our lives and all things to Your divine care.

For God to Make a Way

Make a way for those who call on You.
Heal the broken.
Comfort the grieving.
Bless the dying.
Walk with the weary.

We Give You Praise

Thank You, God:
For Your faithfulness that never fails,
For Your mercy that refreshes us,
For Your provisions that enrich us,
For Your undying love that enlivens us,
For Your loving arms that embrace us,
For Your words that guide us,
For Your eyes that watch over us,
We give You praise.

Tapping into My Superpower

MY PRAYER PETITION

_____

_____

_____

_____

_____

_____

_____

_____

_____

_____

_____

_____

Answered Prayers

\

CALL to REPENTANCE

 If you have not received Jesus as Lord and Savior, we invite you to do so today. Please join us in praying:

Lord Jesus, I confess that I am a sinner. I repent of the things I have said and done that have displeased You. Please forgive me of my sins. I invite Jesus to come into my heart. Begin to renew my mind, cleanse my heart, transform my life. Help me from this day forth, through Your Holy Spirit, to live my life as you direct.

Tapping into Your Superpower

Father, please guide this beloved son or daughter who has just received Your Son as Savior. Keep a watchful eye over Your beloved. Lead Your beloved to the right church, the right pastor who will help develop and strengthen him/her through biblically sound preaching and teaching and mentoring into a disciple for Your honor and glory. Manifest Yourself to Your beloved and allow Your fullest and highest potential for his/her life to be realized. May Your beloved be filled with faith, filled with the Holy Spirit, and daily tap into his/her superpower. In Jesus' name, we pray. Amen.

About the Authors

The Reverend Dr. Joanne J. Noel is an ordained clergywoman, educator, writer, speaker and scholar. Rev. Noel has a Ph.D. in Humanities and Culture from Union Institute and University, a DMIN in practical theology from New Brunswick Seminary, and Masters' degrees in Divinity and English from Rutgers and New Brunswick Seminary. She has more than 20 years of experience in teaching literature, theology, and rhetoric and composition. She has served as interim pastor and is currently on the faculty at Pillar College in New Jersey. She has published various articles, book chapters, and essays in *The ABHE Journal*, *The Department Chair*, *These Sisters Can Say It Too*, *Motivational Moments for Women*, and *The Positive Community*. As an advocate for women's empowerment, she has served as a founding member of the group, Winning Women, an academic and skills-development advocacy group for women as well as Faith Foundation Christian Ministry which provides religious education, life-skills training, and resources to young adults and children in urban schools in the Caribbean. She is an itinerant preacher/teacher/workshop presenter whose call is to preach and teach Kingdom principles to multiple peoples and nations and develop disciples and leaders for academia, the Church, and the marketplace. Her existential purpose is: My highest for his utmost.

Reverend Dr. Maxine A. Bradshaw is the Associate Dean and Professor of Psychology and Counseling in the Master of Arts in Counseling (MAC) and in the Undergraduate Traditional Psychology and Counseling programs at Pillar College. She graduated from the University of the West Indies with a BA in Business with Upper Class Honors and from Howard University where she earned a Master of Arts in Business Administration (MBA), a Master of Education in Counseling (M.Ed.) and a Ph.D. in Counseling Psychology. Dr. Bradshaw is a member and reviewer of the American Association of Colleges and Universities (AACU), serves as a reviewer for the American Association of Colleges for Teacher Education (AACTE) and the International Consortium of Educators (ICED). Her publications include When the Chair becomes the Bully and Understanding Counseling and Psychotherapy. Dr. Bradshaw is a national and international leader, a lecturer, a researcher, a workshop presenter, and a public speaker for churches, organizations, retreats, and conferences. She has received accolades from the Association of Mental Health and Developmental Disabilities (AMHDD) Inc.; The Global Forum for Education and Learning (GFEL) as one of the Top 100 Leaders in Education and Psychology and has been featured in the *Marquis Who's Who* publication as an Educator who demonstrates exceptional achievements in her field who has made notable contributions to society; and as an Outstanding Individual of the Century. Dr. Bradshaw is married to Bishop Marvin Bradshaw Sr., and together, they Pastor Higher Dimensions Ministries Inc. in Newark, NJ.

Dr. Rosette B. Adera has been involved in ministry since high school, where she started and led fellowships and evangelistic teams. She is currently in intercessory ministry, which focuses on the needs of immigrant families. Professionally, she has spent over three decades teaching and working in higher education in Kenya, Canada, and the U.S. She continues to facilitate the inclusion of refugees, new immigrants, and other vulnerable populations into the workforce, as well as academic environments. Dr. Adera currently serves as the Chair of the Business Administration (undergraduate) and MBA in Social Sector Management programs at Pillar College. She also serves on the Board of Garden of Hope Foundation, an initiative that is lifting the lives of youth, women, and children from the slums of Nairobi. Dr. Adera holds a Master of Education from Western University (Canada), a Master's of Arts in Globalization from McMaster University (Canada), and a Doctor of Management in Organizational Behavior from University of Maryland (Global Campus). Dr. Adera's publications include *The Chair as Bully*

(2018), *The Effects of Workplace Bullying on Organizational Climate (2017), Parents: The Logical Link for Supporting Children's Mathematical Understanding (2002).* Dr. Adera is a wife, a mother of two grown children, and a grandmother of one. She and her husband worship and serve at NextGen Church in West Windsor, New Jersey.

 **Deputy Mayor Shelly L. Bell**, is an Empower Proclaim coach who helps women claim their voices and is the Founder and Principal of Shelly Speaks, LLC, a women's development program designed to improve their relationships with God and extend their gifts and callings. Ms. Bell has served as Vice Chair for Somerset County Status on the Commission of Women and as Co-Director for Winning Women, an academic and skills-development advocacy organization for women. Ms. Bell is a renowned religious leader, activist, and political strategist who works at the intersection of faith and politics. She has worked in government and non-profit

sectors for over 15 years and is currently the Regional Political Director for New Jersey Governor Phil Murphy and was instrumental in his re-election to a second term. In her own right, Ms. Bell made history when she became the first African-American to serve on the Township Committee in Montgomery, New Jersey. Ms. Bell is a Distinguished Fellow of Princeton Seminary's Black Theological Leadership Institute and a first-generation college graduate with a B.A. in Psychology and Counseling and an M.A. in Marriage and Family Counseling from Pillar.

Contact the authors at:

TSuperpower4@gmail.com

Please contact Art & Legacy Publications
for your publishing needs:

www.artandlegacypublications.com